WNBA

A Crabtree Branches Book

B. Keith Davidson

CRABTREE
Publishing Company
www.crabtreebooks.com

School-to-Home Support for Caregivers and Teachers

This high-interest book is designed to motivate striving students with engaging topics while building fluency, vocabulary, and an interest in reading. Here are a few questions and activities to help the reader build upon his or her comprehension skills.

Before Reading:

- *What do I think this book is about?*
- *What do I know about this topic?*
- *What do I want to learn about this topic?*
- *Why am I reading this book?*

During Reading:

- *I wonder why...*
- *I'm curious to know...*
- *How is this like something I already know?*
- *What have I learned so far?*

After Reading:

- *What was the author trying to teach me?*
- *What are some details?*
- *How did the photographs and captions help me understand more?*
- *Read the book again and look for the vocabulary words.*
- *What questions do I still have?*

Extension Activities:

- *What was your favorite part of the book? Write a paragraph on it.*
- *Draw a picture of your favorite thing you learned from the book.*

TABLE OF CONTENTS

THE SECOND WOMEN'S LEAGUE

In 1892 women were introduced to the sport of basketball. Over 100 years later, the American Basketball League (ABL), a professional women's league, opened. It was followed soon after by the Women's National Basketball Association (WNBA) which opened its first season in July 1997.

Smith College, in the northeastern United States, was the first college to have a women's basketball team.

Women's basketball uniforms have gone through many changes since 1892. This photo, taken in 1905, shows a team wearing the long skirts required for women basketball players at that time.

The Olympics helped make women's basketball popular. Its popularity after the 1996 Olympic Games in Atlanta led to the opening of both the ABL and the WNBA.

A GAME OF INCHES

Since 1997 the WNBA has been dealing with comparisons to the NBA. The **free-throw line** is closer, the ball is a bit smaller, and the 3-point line is 4 feet (1.2 meters) closer. At first glance, the game might seem easier.

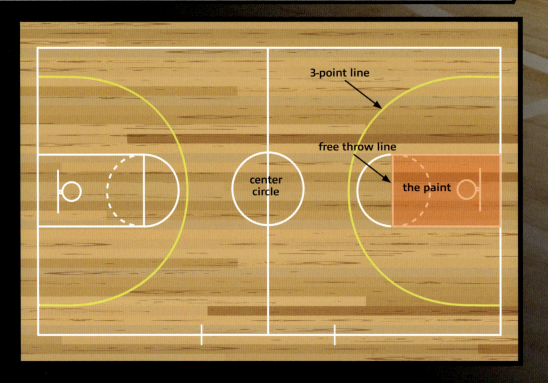

3-point line

free throw line

center circle

the paint

However, the average WNBA player is 6 feet (1.82 meters) tall, and the average NBA player is 6 feet, 7 inches (2 meters) tall. The net for both leagues is 10 feet (3 meters) off the ground, so it seems like the women have it tougher...right?

JUMP BALL

The center's job starts at center court, trying to beat the other team's center to the ball. However, the most important part of her job is performed around the net. The center is there to catch rebounds and dunk on opponents.

Basketball games start at center court with a jump ball.

A QUARTERBACK ON THE COURT

The point guard leads the offense, usually starting from the 3-point line. She has to be good at passing and putting pressure on the defense.

Point guard stars like Ivory Latta (12) don't just look for openings—they make them.

Lindsay Harding had 1,298 points, 25 blocks, 579 assists, 296 steals and 565 rebounds in 128 games (school record) at Duke University.

FEEL THE POWER!

Power forwards are always thinking about scoring, going for **field goals** from any part of the court.

FUN FACT

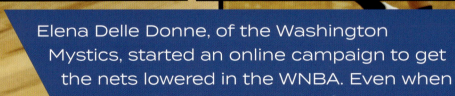

Elena Delle Donne, of the Washington Mystics, started an online campaign to get the nets lowered in the WNBA. Even when they're off the court, power forwards are always thinking about racking up the points!

NOT SO SMALL FORWARDS

Small forwards play a big role in the WNBA. A small forward can be found mixing it up in **the paint**, rebounding the ball, or shooting **3's**. A small forward goes where she is needed.

Margo Dydek, at 7 feet, 2 inches (2.18 m), is the tallest player ever to play in the WNBA. Shannon Bobbit, at 5 feet, 2 inches (1.57 m), is the shortest.

Maya Moore leads the attack for the Minnesota Lynx.

In 2020, the average salary in the WNBA was $100,658. By comparison, the average NBA salary is around $7 million, or about 70 times what the women get paid.

LONG BOMBS

Shooting guards shoot often and shoot from further back in the zone. They are famous for making difficult shots. Shooting guard Diana Taurasi has scored more points than anyone in the league.

FUN FACT

The record for most points in an overtime period is 12. Four women share this special distinction: Mwadi Mabika, Sheryl Swoopes, Deanna Nolan, and Becky Hammon.

Diana Taurasi

SHOOTING FOR THE STARS

There are different types of shots that score points in basketball. **Layups**, dunks, and **jump shots** are all used to score field goals.

THE REFEREES

Most of the rules for the WNBA and the NBA are the same. A player with six personal **fouls** is out of the game. A team that makes eight fouls in one half of a game must give the other team a shot at the free-throw line.

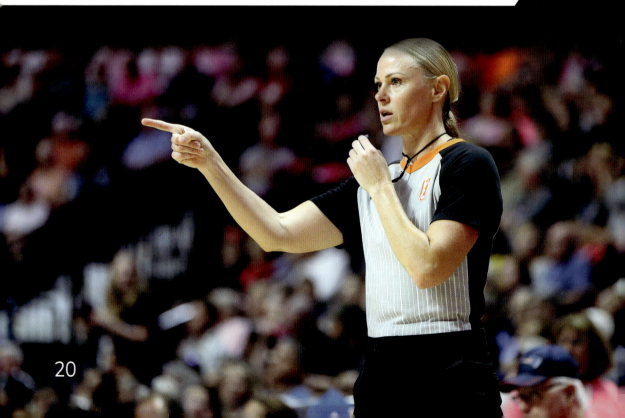

WINNING IT ALL

At the end of the season, the eight best of the twelve WNBA teams compete in the playoffs. These are two rounds of five games. The two winning teams then compete for the championship trophy.

FUN FACT

The record for the most championships is four. The record is shared by the Houston Comets, Minnesota Lynx, and the Seattle Storm.

SHERYL SWOOPES

POSITION

FORWARD GUARD

GAMES PLAYED	324
MINUTES PER GAME	32.7
POINTS PER GAME	15.0
REBOUNDS PER GAME	4.9
ASSISTS PER GAME	3.2

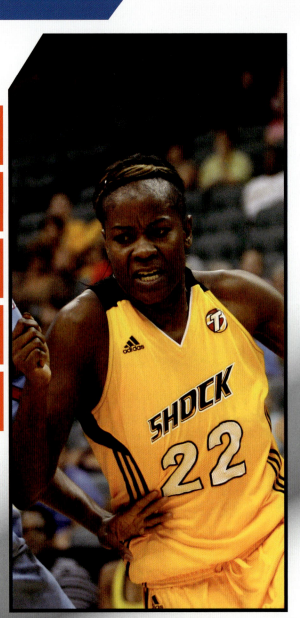

LISA LESLIE

CAREER **1997-2009**

POSITION
CENTER

GAMES PLAYED	**363**
MINUTES PER GAME	**32.0**
POINTS PER GAME	**17.2**
REBOUNDS PER GAME	**9.1**
ASSISTS PER GAME	**2.4**

SUE BIRD

POSITION
GUARD

GAMES PLAYED	**519**
MINUTES PER GAME	**31.7**
POINTS PER GAME	**12.1**
REBOUNDS PER GAME	**2.6**
ASSISTS PER GAME	**5.6**

BRITTNEY GRINER

POSITION
CENTER

GAMES PLAYED	224
MINUTES PER GAME	30.6
POINTS PER GAME	17.3
REBOUNDS PER GAME	7.3
ASSISTS PER GAME	1.7

27

THE WNBA

Women's basketball is played all over the world. It draws big crowds and loyal fans. In North America, the women of the WNBA have earned their place in professional sports entertainment.

GLOSSARY

3's (THREEZ): Three-point field goals made from beyond the three-point line

dunk (DUHNK): To take the ball up to the net and drop it through the rim

field goals (FEELD GOHLZ): Any shot that goes into the net that isn't a free throw

fouls (FOWLZ): Actions in sports that are against the rules

free-throw line (FREE-THROH LINE): The line where a player stands when taking a free throw that resulted from an opponent's foul

jump shots (JUHMP SHOTS): Shots usually taken farther from the hoop and involve jumping while one hand guides the ball and the other hand pushes it forward

layups (LAY-uhps): Shots where the ball is rolled off the fingertips and into the net

rebounds (REE-bowndz): Plays involving catching a ball from a missed shot

the paint (THE PAYNT): Area inside the lane lines from the baseline to the free-throw line

INDEX

COOL FACTS:

Senda Berenson was hired by Smith College in 1892 as the Director of Physical Culture. She was the first person to introduce basketball to female students.

The record for most career points belongs to the Phoenix Mercury's Diana Taurasi with 8,931. Not surprisingly, she also has the record for most points in a season with 860.

Fifty-three is the record for points scored in one game and that honor belongs to Liz Cambage. She did it while playing for the Dallas Wings.

WEBSITES FOR MORE COOL FACTS:

https://kids.kiddle.co/Women%27s_National_
    Basketball_Association

www.hooptactics.net

www.breakthroughbasketball.com/coaching/
    youthbasketball.html

ABOUT THE AUTHOR

B. Keith Davidson

B. Keith Davidson grew up playing with his three brothers and a host of neighborhood children, learning about life through sports and physical activity. He now teaches these games to his three children.

We recognize that some words, team names, and designations, for example, mentioned herein are the property of the trademark holder. We use them for identification purposes only. This is not an official publication.

CRABTREE
Publishing Company

Produced by: Blue Door Education for Crabtree Publishing

Written by: B. Keith Davidson

Designed by: Jennifer Dydyk

Edited by: Tracy Nelson Maurer

Proofreader: Ellen Rodger

Photographs: Cover: Background photo © Shutterstock.com/ Oleksii Sidorov, players © Kathy Willens / Associated Press, PG 4-5: Courtesy of the Library of Congress, PG 6: ©shutterstock.com/Anucha Tiemsom, PG 7: ©Danny Raustadt| Dreamstime.com (all), PG 8: ©Danny Raustadt| Dreamstime.com, PG 9: ©Danny Raustadt| Dreamstime.com, PG 10: ©Tony Quinn /Associated Press, PG 11: ©Keeton10| Dreamstime.com, PG 12: ©Keeton Gale / Shutterstock.com, PG 13: ©Danny Raustadt| Dreamstime.com, PG 14: ©Danny Raustadt| Dreamstime.com, PG 15: ©Keeton10| Dreamstime.com, PG 17: ©Keeton Gale / Shutterstock.com, PG 18: ©Keeton10| Dreamstime.com, PG 19: ©Danny Raustadt| Dreamstime.com, PG 20: ©Mingo Nesmith/Icon Sportswire/Associated Press, PG 21: ©Leslie Banks| Dreamstime.com, ©Danny Raustadt| Dreamstime.com (inset), PG 22: ©Chris O'Meara/ Associated Press, PG 23: ©Alex Brandon/ Associated Press, PG 24: ©Sue Ogrocki/ Associated Press, PG 25: ©Gus Ruelas/ Associated Press, PG 26: ©Phelan M. Ebenhack/ Associated Press, PG 27: ©Keeton10| Dreamstime.com, PG 28: © Igor Panevski / Shutterstock.com, PG 29: © Dmitry Argunov| Dreamstime.com

Library and Archives Canada Cataloguing in Publication

Title: WNBA / B. Keith Davidson.
Other titles: Women's National Basketball Association
Names: Davidson, B. Keith, 1982- author.
Description: Series statement: Major league sports |
    "A Crabtree branches book." | Includes index.
Identifiers: Canadiana (print) 20210220368 |
    Canadiana (ebook) 20210220376 |
    ISBN 9781427155238 (hardcover) |
    ISBN 9781427155290 (softcover) |
    ISBN 9781427155351 (HTML) |
    ISBN 9781427155412 (EPUB) |
    ISBN 9781427155474 (read-along ebook)
Subjects: LCSH: Women's National Basketball Association—
    Juvenile literature. | LCSH: Basketball for women—
    United States—Juvenile literature.
Classification: LCC GV885.515.W66 D38 2022 | DDC j796.323/
    64082—dc23

Library of Congress Cataloging-in-Publication Data

Names: Davidson, B. Keith, 1982- author.
Title: WNBA B. Keith Davidson.
Other titles: Women's National Basketball Association
Description: New York : Crabtree Publishing Company, 2022. |
    Series: Major league sports | "A Crabtree Branches Book".
Identifiers: LCCN 2021022562 (print) |
    LCCN 2021022563 (ebook) |
    ISBN 9781427155238 (hardcover) |
    ISBN 9781427155290 (paperback) |
    ISBN 9781427155351 (ebook) |
    ISBN 9781427155412 (epub) |
    ISBN 9781427155474
Subjects: LCSH: Women's National Basketball Association--History--Juvenile literature. | Women's basketball--United States--History--Juvenile literature.
Classification: LCC GV885.515.W66 D38 2022 (print) | LCC GV885.515.W66 (ebook) | DDC 796.323082--dc23
LC record available at https://lccn.loc.gov/2021022562
LC ebook record available at https://lccn.loc.gov/2021022563

Crabtree Publishing Company

www.crabtreebooks.com   1-800-387-7650

Printed in the U.S.A./072021/CG20210514

Published in the United States
Crabtree Publishing
347 Fifth Avenue, Suite 1402-145
New York, NY, 10016

Published in Canada
Crabtree Publishing
616 Welland Ave.
St. Catharines, ON, L2M 5V6